CREEPY CRAWLIES

Mealworms

by Kari Schuetz

BELLWETHER MEDIA • MINNEAPOLIS, MN

Note to Librarians, Teachers, and Parents:

Blastoff! Readers are carefully developed by literacy experts and combine standards-based content with developmentally appropriate text.

Level 1 provides the most support through repetition of high-frequency words, light text, predictable sentence patterns, and strong visual support.

Level 2 offers early readers a bit more challenge through varied simple sentences, increased text load, and less repetition of high-frequency words.

Level 3 advances early-fluent readers toward fluency through increased text and concept load, less reliance on visuals, longer sentences, and more literary language.

Level 4 builds reading stamina by providing more text per page, increased use of punctuation, greater variation in sentence patterns, and increasingly challenging vocabulary.

Level 5 encourages children to move from "learning to read" to "reading to learn" by providing even more text, varied writing styles, and less familiar topics.

Whichever book is right for your reader, Blastoff! Readers are the perfect books to build confidence and encourage a love of reading that will last a lifetime!

This edition first published in 2016 by Bellwether Media, Inc.

No part of this publication may be reproduced in whole or in part without written permission of the publisher. For information regarding permission, write to Bellwether Media, Inc., Attention: Permissions Department, 5357 Penn Avenue South, Minneapolis, MN 55419.

Library of Congress Cataloging-in-Publication Data

Schuetz, Kari, author.
 Mealworms / by Kari Schuetz.
   pages cm. – (Blastoff! Readers. Creepy Crawlies)
 Summary: "Developed by literacy experts for students in kindergarten through grade three, this book introduces mealworms to young readers through leveled text and related photos"– Provided by publisher.
 Audience: Ages 5-8
 Audience: K to grade 3
 Includes bibliographical references and index.
 ISBN 978-1-62617-224-1 (hardcover: alk. paper)
 1. Meal worms–Juvenile literature. I. Title. II. Title: Meal worms.
 QL596.T2S375 2016
 595.76′9–dc23
                       2015005966

Printed in the United States of America, North Mankato, MN.

Table of Contents

Baby Beetles

Mealworms are baby **insects**. They grow up to be darkling beetles.

The little **grubs** are called **larvae**. They **hatch** from eggs.

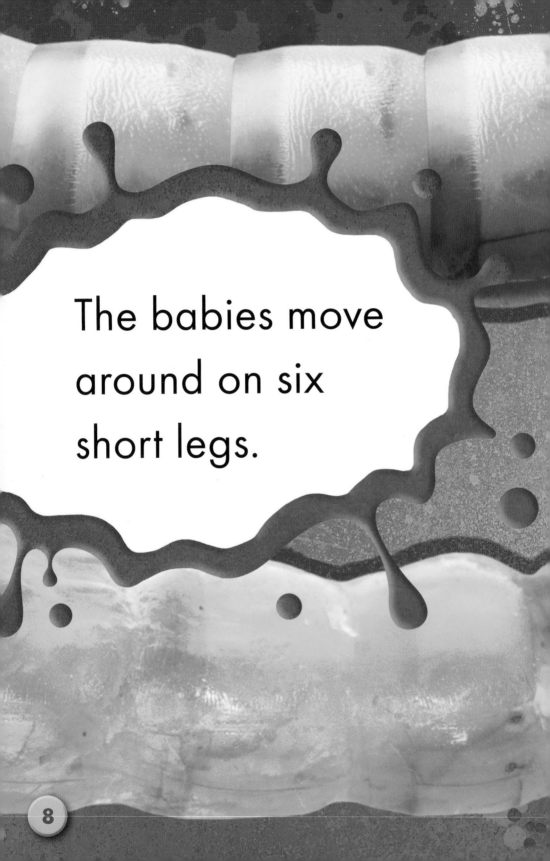

The babies move
around on six
short legs.

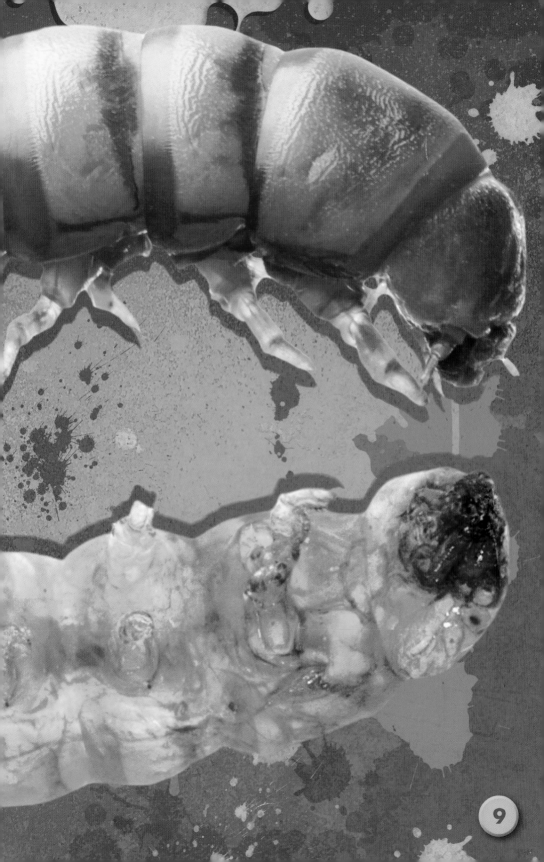

Changing Color

Mealworms have
a hard outer skin.
This layer is brown.

They **molt** this
skin many times.
Their new skin
is always soft
and white.

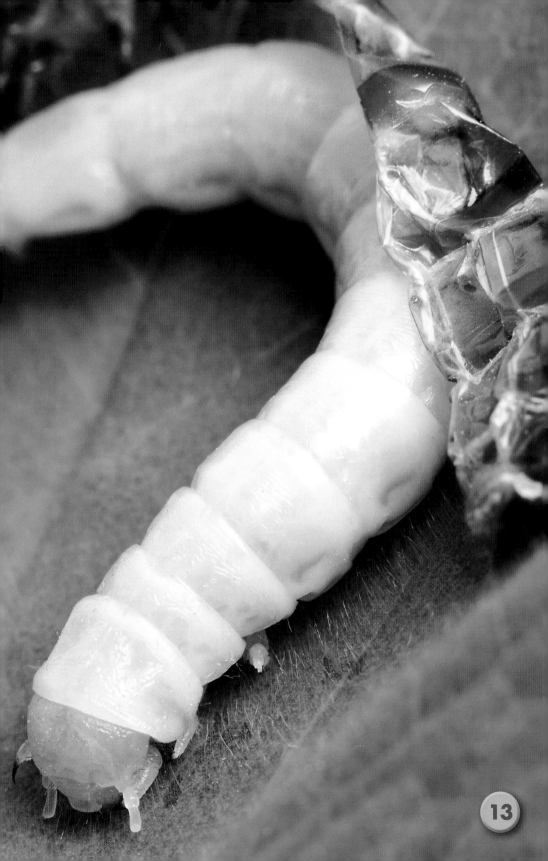

Eating to Grow

Mealworms must eat a lot to grow. Their menu includes **grains** and dead insects.

15

They look for food under rocks and in animal **burrows**.

Sometimes mealworms become dinner. Birds and spiders eat them.

Pupae, Then Adults

Within weeks, mealworms turn into wiggling **pupae**. Then they become adults!

pupa

adult

Glossary

burrows—holes or tunnels that some animals dig in the ground

grains—seeds of food plants

grubs—baby beetles

hatch—to break out of an egg

insects—small animals with six legs and hard outer bodies; an insect's body is divided into three parts.

larvae—baby insects that have hatched from eggs; larvae look like worms.

molt—to shed skin

pupae—young insects that are about to become adults

To Learn More

AT THE LIBRARY
Jenkins, Steve. *The Beetle Book*. Boston, Mass.: Houghton Mifflin Books for Children, 2012.

Rustad, Martha E.H. *Mealworms*. Mankato, Minn.: Capstone Press, 2009.

Salas, Laura Purdie. *From Mealworm to Beetle: Following the Life Cycle*. Minneapolis, Minn.: Picture Window Books, 2009.

ON THE WEB
Learning more about mealworms is as easy as 1, 2, 3.

1. Go to www.factsurfer.com.

2. Enter "mealworms" into the search box.

3. Click the "Surf" button and you will see a list of related web sites.

With factsurfer.com, finding more information is just a click away.

Index

The images in this book are reproduced through the courtesy of: Michiel de Wit, front cover (large); schankz, front cover (small top); Anneka, front cover (small bottom); Anatolich, p. 5; Artit Fongfung, p. 7; Eric Isselee, pp. 9 (top), 21 (top); Pan Xunbin, p. 9 (bottom); wawritto, p. 11; Photowitch, p. 13; Nigel Cattlin/ Alamy, p. 15; Aleksandar Todorovic, p. 17; Steve Byland, p. 19; Akil Rolle-Rowan, p. 21 (bottom).